Land

Of

Souls

Where The Light of Shadows Fall

The Poetry Alliance

Land Of Souls: Where the Light of Shadows Fall

Printed in the United States of America

ISBN-13:978-0692305997
ISBN-10:0692305998

Printed by Createspace 2014

Published by BlaqRayn Publishing in 2014

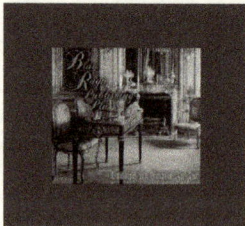

The Poetry Alliance Authors

Ken Blick

Elluisa Granath–Vargas Conroy

Rose Mary McKenzie

Thaddeus Hutyra

Ryan Christiano

Linde Griffis

Alyson Rewick

Ana Vargas

Joy Blevins

Introduction

Elluisa Conroy and Ken Blick had friends in common. Ken was posting his poetry in FaceBook poetry groups and Elluisa, an avid reader and lover of poetry, started commenting on his beautifully written work. As these communications continued, Ken and Elluisa found they shared a passion for writing and decided to create their own poetry community.

Together they created **The Poetry Alliance**, bringing in others having a similar passion for writing and poetry. Collectively as a group, their dream had always been to be published.

Now their dream is a reality.

Land

Of

Souls

WHERE THE LIGHT OF SHADOWS FALL

The Poetry Alliance

Elluisa Granath-

Vargas Conroy

Yearning

Will my heart ever dance

or feel love again?

will I always have these tears built

deep inside? Will I ever get another chance?

The more I try

the more I get shot down

wondering if he's out there? Does he even see me

does he know I exist? The one I speak of, the king

with a crown.

The one looking for his queen

All this hurt is just so obscene.

Will I ever dance in the rain?

Or will I forever feel this pain?

If you're out there and it is I you seek

tug at my hand and show me

Or is what I am looking for

exist or am I only speaking Greek?

So tattered and torn

how much longer

must I morn?
I am doing my best to
stand and be stronger.

With all the lies
how can one stand a float?
or to keep trying, please
send me a rescue boat.

Mistakes

Not sure how much more I can take

I look above and think Heavens sake

How many more am I going to make?

So tired of all these mistakes.

Where to find the words to truly heal,

When will it be time to truly feel?

Not just to be taken one fancy meal,

I want a make this an official seal.

So tired of being lost and broken,

With no words to be spoken,

Just another dropped token.

How my heart has been stolen,

So confused on how to keep things rolling.

Trying to stay above and feel like sinking,

Everything has kept me thinking,

Hope this problem would keep shrinking,

Instead it leaves me tattered, torn, and blinking.

Before You Rest

You carried me

gave me life

showed me love

even when there was strife.

Taught me from wrong

also right

always gave me hugs

as you kissed and tucked me in at night.

Always there

through good and bad

always wiping the tears

from being sad.

Never forget the way

you glued cotton balls

on my sunglasses, I was so mad

as I watched you laugh down the hall.

Best of the best

worked so hard

even remember you working

in the yard.

Humble and always caring

such a beautiful smile

I hope and pray I get to have

you around for a long while.

All the things you

had to endure

but looked at all the positive

you had in store.

It clearly shows

that you try your best

I had to show you I care before we ever

lay you down to rest.

TIME STANDS STILL

As time stands still

With tunes of

Rhythm and blues,

Dressed in tie dye and good ole body glove,

While dancing to my blue suede shoe.

Hearts are racing full of fire,

Oh baby can't you see my desire?

The pulse in my heart,

Oh God just to look in your eye

Fresh at the start.

Looking deep into your eyes

wanting to feel your embrace.

As time stands still,

Wishing to be in your grace.

Time lingers on

my heart wanting more

As time stands still

I'm laying here on the floor.

WHERE THE LIGHT OF SHADOWS FALL

Is this how it will

Forever be?

Will one ever see?

Must time just stand still?

LOST

There are times in our life

Were we feel lost and

Out of place with needing

Some much needed space.

Confusion of not knowing

Up or down and spinning all around

Spinning in constant circles trying to hold

On gripping tight just to keep you on solid ground.

Trying to find yourself

Digging really deep

All you see is darkness it wraps you tight

Suffocating you and making you weep.

You look to the lord above

Ask for a sign, all of a sudden there is a dove

Another sign of Gods sweet precious

Tender love.

MIXED EMOTIONS

Mixed Emotions

So much hurt I feel deep inside

Taken on a ownership with

A dear friend. Being treated

Non existent, and wanting to hide.

These feelings are so deep

When I think of how he's made

Me feel and doesn't seem to care

Makes me weep at night before going to sleep.

I often feel he doesn't care

Putting others in charge with out a word, I hold it all deep

inside

I want to approach but I don't dare.

I feel our creation is reaching an end, for he's taken on too

much

So we sit quietly with nothing going on. With so much to try

and mend.

I often wonder if he knows the pain

That lays deep inside or even know

How he's made me feel? Will this group survive or end up

down the drain?

Trying to pull it through

But kind of hard when I think

About leaving without a word or notice as I sit and stew.

Asking to be treated more fair

I thought we were in this together

Equally at the start,   a dream of ours

Now I glance from a distance and stare.

With mixed emotions full of hurt

As I wonder why or what I have done,

To be treated like this and

To feel like dirt.

BROKEN PROMISES

So tired of broken promises
All the hurt and betrayal
Sick of the train and the road
That has been derailed.

Why must I go through
All of this pain?
Trying so hard to stay focused
Most of all sane.

Will my heart ever dance
Or feel love again?
Will I always have these tears built
Deep inside? Will I ever get another chance?

The more I try the more I get shot down
Wondering if he is out there? Does he even see me
Does he know I exists? The one I speak of the king with a
crown.

The one looking for his queen.
All this hurt is just so obscene.
Will I dance again in the rain?

WHERE THE LIGHT OF SHADOWS FALL

Or will I forever feel this pain?

If your out there and it i you seek
Tug at my hand an show me
Or is what I am looking for
Only speaking in Greek?

So tattered and torn
How much longer
Must I morn?
I am doing my best to
Stand and be stronger.

With all the flies
How can one stand a float
Or to keep on trying?

LIFE CHANGES

Life Changes
Sitting here in the dark
Thinking of child hood days
Of all the fun
While   being at the park.

Days so bright
Where time has gone
Completely down hill
With losing sight.

So many have be taken away
How I miss and love them
Every single day. At least I know
They're   in Heaven to stay.

Often think what's ahead for me
Staying focused can be hard
Yearning for love
Wonder if love will ever truly be?

Feeling so lost with emotions
Trying to do my best

To keep stepping
Following all the notions.

Doing my best trying to find me
Will things change?
Maybe brighter?
Will I ever be able to fully see?

Funny how life changes
Just when you think you have it
Figured   out boom all of a sudden
There you are as it rearranges.

DREAMS OF YOU

Dreams of you

With dreams of you holding me tight

Trying to give love another fight

Being safe within your arms

Finally safe from all the harm.

This feeling is so strong

I can't fight it this feeling

There is no way this is wrong

I can feel you and my heart you're stealing

All these strong emotions

How you've caught my heart

Caressing my fears as if it were lotion

Looking forward to this new start.

As I place my hand

Watching things blossom

Like writing in the sand

This feeling is just so awesome.

With dreams of you

I hold you tight

WHERE THE LIGHT OF SHADOWS FALL

This is too good to be true
Waking to the morning light.

With dreams of falling in love
Our hearts together as one
Fitting together like a glove
No more of being on the run.

For you've captured my dream
You've got my heart
Love flowing like an endless stream
Praying I continue to do my part.

Thaddeus

Hutyra

Lovers of Universe

You're in my arms, we're in the arms of stars

dancing together in the starlight

while passionately kissing each other

Our kisses are formed of interstellar dust

our love is threaded of rays from the stars

and we're continuing to kiss one another

we, the amaranthine lovers of Universe

And though we're standing on a beach

in the embrace of moonlighted night

chatting in a New York cafe

till the late night hours

or speeding up a car direction California

we're embraced as much by the stars

shining us brilliantly from the luminous sky

Though we're sitting on dangerous cliffs

overlooking the powers of the Poseidon's sea

no matter whether together

or far away from one another

we're still the galactic adventurers

guardians of Universe in love

WHERE THE LIGHT OF SHADOWS FALL

The echoes of our deep love
spread fast across Scottish land masses
across the Alps, across Carpathians
across mountains of the Caucasus
flying like a mysterious jet plane
and ending somewhere there in China
still being echoed from a wall to a wall
of the ancient Chinese Wall

There is no rest to our passionate love
'cause we are brought on our starship
into furthest dimensions of the many galactics
dancing our love in the never ending starlit space
singing our love to the tunes of various sounds of Universe
and kissing each other with the energy
borrowed from the stars
no need really to return what's borrowed

Oh, my darling, we're destined for each other
never to be split, always together
even if the winds bring us far apart
even if fate not always is favorable
yet we're acquiescent to whatever might happen
'cause we know nothing can split us

WHERE THE LIGHT OF SHADOWS FALL

We're simply dancing in the arms of stars
dancing together in the starlight
while passionately kissing each other
Our kisses are formed of interstellar dust
our love is threaded of rays from the stars
and we're continuing to kiss one another
we, the amaranthine lovers of Universe

No matter what happens we're together
no matter where you are or I am we're together
Tolstoy's War and Peace, Shakespeare's Hamlet
The Bells brought to life by Edgar Allan Poe
Whatever it might be we're together
destined to one another, married by our love
'cause our love is one, one and only one
'cause our souls are one soul, our hearts are one heart
'cause our desires are one desire, our desire
'cause all we are are two halves being whole
'cause our spirits are mixed by wand of love
into elixir, the elixir of love

Wow, we're dancing in adrenalized Tomorrowland
dancing in Amsterdam's Arena at Sensation White
dancing frenziedly in New York's Boulevard
on Mount Victoria in windy Wellington's starry night
dancing among stars, we, the lovers of Universe !!

WHERE THE LIGHT OF SHADOWS FALL

Earth and stars are the fields of our love

we're the lovers since Adam and Eve

the amaranthine lovers of Universe

drinking elixirs of love from our lips

elixirs which form us all to who we are

we, the lovers of Universe, forevermore.

Angel of the Day

Lost angel of the day

falling down from the blue sky

Poor angel tries to catch the rays

the way as spiders are doing it

by forming celestial spiderwebs

one after another one

from the rays of the sunshine

Spiderwebs follow spiderwebs

but seem to be too weak to hold

the weight of the angel

The effects are effulgent displays

of the Sun's rays

as if Mozart played his best

Millions and millions

billions even and billions

of the celestial cobwebs

threaded out of the Sun's rays

seen and heard

as a symphony of skies

symphony of Heavens

gifted to the human kind

WHERE THE LIGHT OF SHADOWS FALL

And among the brilliant threads
the angel of the day
catching each thread
but falling and falling
He can already be seen
by a naked eye
certainly by the eagle eye

Fallen though
the angel hits the ground
Wings broken
unable to fly back
where his home to
How incongruous is his new situation
among those calling themselves humans
too rude to each other
using means of force too easily
murdering even
as if with no soul
no humanity
no feelings
no values

Lost angel of the day
has no other choice
as to get rid of his heavenly wings

and walk towards those

calling themselves humans

His heartbeat is nearly getting to its stop

out of agony

out of stress

out of fear

out of the knowledge it's not his place

strange and ruthless

so much unlike Heavens

although not yet as hell

Yet once among humans

he has a chance

to see through different windows of reality

unlike the window to Heavens

This world is built on relative standards

what's true for some

untrue for others

what's rightful to some

unacceptable to others

what are the norms to be followed for some

never to be followed by others

contradicted with their own norms

clash of civilizations

He runs out onto a field

filled with symphonic rays of the Sun

and orchestral performance

of both Earth and the sky

He opens his arms

out of sheer despair

and â€¦ bewilderment

'cause the heartbeat of this world

becomes his own heartbeat

as if a mysterious sorcerer

threw a curse on him

No, he is not cursed by Heavens

no, this never can't !!

What a transformation !

He knows it all now

all the things concerning humans

He feels them all

he feels it all

love

desires

strivings to happiness

in spite of all miseries

determinations to change this world

and let goodness to win over evil

soulfulness of men and women

trying their best

being fathers and mothers

not only lovers

The heartbeat of the world

beats in accordance with his own heartbeat

Earth and Heavens seem to be united

at least for the moment

all this love

all those romances

all those smiles

all those yearnings

all those whispers

all those embraces

all those family meetings

all those church attendances

and bells sparkling, twinkling and ringing

The next sequence is altogether different

He, the angel of the day

is rescued by fellow angels

Rising into the sky

and far beyond

He feels his heartbeat

filled with love

towards those calling themselves humans

despite their flaws

There is finally nothing else left

but a music of the Sun's rays

conducted by him

the invisible angel this time

angel of the day.

Ode to Life

Dear Life, you're the embodiment
of the very best, a bell of bells
the Bell of Life, cementing all bells
the bell of liberty, enlightenment
desires to be free and live in dignity
the bell of all the great times in life
displaying thousands and one bells
accumulated in one, the Bell of Life
ringing brilliantly across the globe
and announcing like Archangel Michael
the victory of all people of goodwill
over the vicious tyrannies of darkness
and the resurrection of life forever
You're the king of all seasons, dear Life
and of this fabulous Spring right now

Oh, bells, bells, ring my bells
Oh, amber and diamond bells
ring and ring, bring a toast to life
cause people reach high spirits
and dance throughout their lives
cause life is forever, most dear of all

XXIX

Dear Life, you're a music to our ears
a Leonardo Da Vinci's painting
a film Scorsese never dreamed about
You're a symphony of Mozart
Beethoven and other masters
the Symphony of perpetual Life
You're a musical of all times
The Phantom of the Opera
Cleopatra, Cats, Les Misérables
You're virginious Chorus of Angels
singing for you heavenly, divinely
You're the people of the world
from those living in the forgotten
small and poor, far away villages
to those living in big cities
and enjoying spectacular city lights
Yet the world is a global village !

Oh, bells, bells, ring my bells
Oh, amber and diamond bells
ring and ring, bring a toast to life
cause people reach high spirits
and dance throughout their lives
cause life is forever, most dear of all

XXX

WHERE THE LIGHT OF SHADOWS FALL

Dear Life, the most precious jewel
you're everlasting set of seasons
Seasons of Life, the true elixirs
Spring, the season of Youth
life–giving, thunderstorm alike
Summer, the early adult season
promiscuous, burning with Love
the adventurous Love full of Erotics
Love so rich like the shining stars
stars on fire, the Stars of Love
Autumn, the golden season
of splendid family responsibilities
and as much professional ones
the Autumn of Life, indeed
and finally, the Winter season
when one is on a deserved pension
and the wheel of life slows down

Oh, bells, bells, ring my bells
Oh, amber and diamond bells
ring and ring, bring a toast to life
cause people reach high spirits
and dance throughout their lives
cause life is forever, most dear of all

WHERE THE LIGHT OF SHADOWS FALL

Dear Life, you're the embodiment
of greatest ever love story come true
You are giving us a godlike chance
to live an everlasting Circle of Life
throughout our adventurous lives
sharing it and as much our love
with the love ones, our friends
and all the other people of goodwill
Letting the wheel of life, God's wheel
to take a full, 360 degrees swing
till we can finally bid a farewell
You are guiding us endlessly
throughout our turbulent lives
like the shiny Star of Bethlehem
which guided Our Virgin Mary
and Saint Joseph away from Herod

Oh, bells, bells, ring my bells
Oh, amber and diamond bells
ring and ring, bring a toast to life
cause people reach high spirits
and dance throughout their lives
cause life is forever, most dear of all

Dear Life, you're the greatest of elixirs
the unprecedented Elixir of Life

never discovered and though
existent in each of us, our essence
The essence as much of our souls
the Souls of Life, making us immortal
You're our Guardian of the Universe
on this planet Earth, our home
Each of us must go away one day
or one night, on a celestial trip
with a farewell sealed on our lips
Yet we all know it quite good
the Circle of Life stays forever on
turning the Wheel of Life, God's Wheel
on and on, and on, till the eternity

Oh, bells, bells, ring my bells
Oh, amber and diamond bells
ring and ring, bring a toast to life
cause people reach high spirits
and dance throughout their lives
cause life is forever, most dear of all.

New York, New York

Look at Manhattan, the Center of the Universe
fabulous beyond anything to say, breathtaking
Look at Times Square, the World's Crossroads
the hub of the Broadway theatre district
Look at the skyscrapers reaching heavens
at the financial center in the Wall Street
the spectacular New York's Stock Exchange
at Manhattan's Chinatown, at the subway
at the Freedom Tower, the pearl of pearls
express your utmost wonder, delight yourself
See New Yorkers hurrying to their jobs
cheerful, optimistic, exuberant, self−confident
See a handsome man walking down the street
see a beautiful woman in red sitting on a bench
a shiny pearl among the busy human traffic
See him approaching her and gently kissing her
see them dancing their tango, the tango of love
among the yellow cabs and Manhattan limousines

*

WHERE THE LIGHT OF SHADOWS FALL

Look at Central Park, the New York's lungs
and the godlike splendor of the nature there
emanating from all corners and at all seasons
in the very heart of marvelous New York City
Look at those millions of people, proud Americans
descendants from all corners of the globe
doing their best to be part of the American Dream
Oh, God bless America, God bless the whole world !!
See happy and carefree kids in Central Park
playing with the plentiful rays from the Sun
and with palette of many shadows from Earth
in the full blown triumphant Summer around
and magnificent scents generated by the trees
What a splendid playground, a symphony it is
a heavenly music to the tunes of the Sun's harp
and yes, the Sun's trumpet, Sun's violin
the Sun's saxophone, all the divine Sun's tools
and of course, the Earth's piano as well
a music larger than life, at kids' hands

*

Majestic New York, you, the Tower of Babel
New York, New York, you, the Spectacle of Life
New York, New York, you, the Symphony of Love
New York, New York, my only City, my love

WHERE THE LIGHT OF SHADOWS FALL

New York, New York, the City we all love

New York, New York, you, the jewel of all jewels

The everlasting Spring and the Summer's sunshine

New York, New York, majestic New York

*

See the Bronx, Brooklyn, Manhattan

picturesque Queens and Staten Island

the jewels of America, of the world as much

See the magnificent Hudson River

emptying into Upper New York Bay

Yankee Stadium, home of the New York Yankees

the Bronx Zoo, the world's largest metropolitan one

the John F. Kennedy International Airport

Thousand and one wonders, indeed

Once New Amsterdam, turned New York City

shining like the Sun on a brightest day

and like shimmering stars at quiet nights

like the ecstasy of men and women in love

a pearl in the crown of America, indeed

kept safely in the claws of the American hawk

Look at all those busy people of New York yet again

making their dreams come true

Oh, New Yorkers, New Yorkers

you're the vanguard of the world !

You're shooting for the stars !!

WHERE THE LIGHT OF SHADOWS FALL

*

New York City, you're our Ode to Life

you're our everlasting Bell of Life

our Dreamland which came true

our Highway to Heavens, a reborn Soul

our Happy End at our final Crossroads

the brilliant diamond, amber and emerald

You're mesmerizingly All American

a hauntingly fabulous Mirror of the World

and the shining Jewel of the Free World

Oh, New York, the true Tower of Babel

my love, our love, forevermore !!

Let's finally look at the Statue of Liberty

whoever you are

She's our Light as much as New York is

reminding us every single moment of our lives

freedom is what counts

and what is worth to strive for

The Statue of Liberty

standing there triumphantly

at the gate to everlasting New York City

*

WHERE THE LIGHT OF SHADOWS FALL

Majestic New York, you, the Tower of Babel

New York, New York, you, the Spectacle of Life

New York, New York, you, the Symphony of Love

New York, New York, my only City, my love

New York, New York, the City we all love

New York, New York, you, the jewel of all jewels

New York, New York, the Fall's and Winter's brilliance

New York, New York, majestic New York.

Sleepless Poet

What a thrilling Wrath of God was it

in the very blackness of the night

turned to a luminous whiteness from time to time !!

Hail, hail and hail, pellets of frozen rain

falling in showers from cumulonimbus clouds

all of them of the size of tennis balls

In the very Summer. Was it not appalling ?!

They were falling from the dark abyss of the sky

which was wholly overwhelmed by stormy clouds

being shown in all their royal majesty

every time the lightnings zigzagged

across the vast spaces of heavenly space

followed by new, powerful thunderstorms

a dance of the lightnings and thunderstorms, indeed

and of the hailstorm changing the scenaries

of New York City constantly, the whole long night

In that deepness of the super stormy night

a poet was sitting at the window

of his apartment, just opposite MoMa

the Museum of Modern Art on 53rd Street

This museum of the adamantine ladies

looked extremely ghostly in the stormy night
The street was covered by many levels
of balls of hails upon hails, shining, glittering
reflecting lots of amaranthine light
in the city lights and at storm's lightnings
as if they were some real diamonds
miraculously spread all over the place
some ambers, emeralds and pearls
all the other precious stones one could imagine
and the modern civilizations were mad for

Oh, you the true poet, the poet of New York City
reach for a pen, your scintillating wand
and a starlit star–ship capable to travel
across vast universes upon universes
and the inner worlds where our souls stay
Change this world, dear poet of New York City
for a better one, more human, cherishing freedoms
May the celestial symphony adds music of liberation
to all your efforts, my dear poet of New York
Oh, phantoms, phantoms, my beloved phantoms
phantoms of the Universe and phantoms of this Earth
phantoms of the Day and of the Night
phantoms of poetry, of arts, of creation
phantoms of love, of desire, of heart
Inspire this poet, bring him to the tops

of his creative skills and let him create

amaranthine masterpiece of sparkling poetry

bring then this on the tray before the very God

Appease Him. No more Wrath of God !!

There was lots of rain water which was streaming

down the typical New York City windows

sometimes seeming to be dark red

as if blood of innocents were spurting out

somewhere else in the wider world

being projected for New Yorkers

The lightnings in the blackness of the night

looked so incredibly surrealistic

as if this was some outer world

Yet they were real ones, and photogenic

as if they were phantoms of the light

phantoms of the ghost, or soul on the lose

phantoms of the night and of the dance

whatever other scintillating phantoms

having their fun in the blackness of the night

The poet remembered what Barack Obama said

when commenting on Russian actions in Crimea

The days of empires taking on their smaller nations

were definitely over, not acceptable, never again

America shall never allow the ghosts of the past

to take over the twenty first century
desired to be a century of justice for all
of flourishing freedoms and of democratic ideas
It was a remark clearly stated against Putin
the guy who thought he could do anything
what he wanted, in a clear disregard
of the world's dream, wish and determination
to move beyond all the evils of the past
and spread freedoms and light of liberty
across the entire troubled globe, needing this much

Oh, you the true poet, the poet of New York City
reach for a pen, your scintillating wand
and a starlit star–ship capable to travel
across vast universes upon universes
and the inner worlds where our souls stay
Change this world, dear poet of New York City
for a better one, more human, cherishing freedoms
May the celestial symphony adds music of liberation
to all your efforts, my dear poet of New York
Oh, phantoms, phantoms, my beloved phantoms
phantoms of the Universe and phantoms of this Earth
phantoms of the Day and of the Night
phantoms of poetry, of arts, of creation
phantoms of love, of desire, of heart
Inspire this poet, bring him to the tops

of his creative skills and let him create

amaranthine masterpiece of sparkling poetry

bring then this on the tray before the very God

Appease Him. No more Wrath of God !!

The lightnings went on, a dance of the hailstorm

in the blackness of the phantoms' night

Phantoms of the ghost, of the dance

appeared from time to time, disappearing then

The poet was still sitting at the window

watching all those phenomenons of nature

fascinated especially by the lightnings on the sky

and the Wrath of God, so visible

Just this night, in the blackness of the night

everything seemed to have come to life

the thunderous lightnings waking them up

waking up even all the ghosts hidden so far

within the walls of the Museum of the Modern Art

just across the street. How phenomenal !!

Whatever there was in rushed cheerfully outside

to celebrate their unchained freedom

while the Wrath of God on human kind went on

The poet looked like hypnotized at this museum

and couldn't believe at all what he saw

It must have been Beethoven's Appassionata

transformed into figurative display

of all those famous masterpieces of art

on the parade to please God and dancing angels

the Virgins of Avignon by Pablo Picasso

the Bather of Paul Cézanne

the Starry Night by Vincent van Gogh

the Seed of the Areoi by Paul Gauguin

the Sleeping Gypsy by Henri Rousseau

God, so many wonders, all eternal ones

The poet couldn't really take his eyes away

from all those wonders upon wonders of human hand

Oh, you the true poet, the poet of New York City

reach for a pen, your scintillating wand

and a starlit star-ship capable to travel

across vast universes upon universes

and the inner worlds where our souls stay

Change this world, dear poet of New York City

for a better one, more human, cherishing freedoms

May the celestial symphony adds music of liberation

to all your efforts, my dear poet of New York

Oh, phantoms, phantoms, my beloved phantoms

phantoms of the Universe and phantoms of this Earth

phantoms of the Day and of the Night

phantoms of poetry, of arts, of creation

phantoms of love, of desire, of heart

WHERE THE LIGHT OF SHADOWS FALL

Inspire this poet, bring him to the tops
of his creative skills and let him create
amaranthine masterpiece of sparkling poetry
bring then this on the tray before the very God
Appease Him. No more Wrath of God !!

The poet rushed through his messy apartment
messy in a positive way cos it was artistic mess
He picked up his Johnny Walker and rushed back
to be a witness to things larger than life
There was the Man with a Guitar by Georges Braque
the Dance by Henri Matisse, the Dream by Henri Rousseau
Pablo Picasso's Boy Leading a Horse
Broadway Boogie-Woogie by Piet Mondrian
Gold Marilyn Monroe by Andy Warhol
Thousands of tinkling and twinkling art masterpieces
given their chance to live their night
while the round formed hails where bouncing
from windows to windows, landing then
on each other on the street, with multiple levels
shining like the Earthly stars vice heavenly stars
every time thunderstorms were followed
by the God's lightnings across the stormy skies

The poet didn't really need much time
to get firmly embraced by overwhelming euphoria

WHERE THE LIGHT OF SHADOWS FALL

He just stood up and began to dance
to the tunes of the thrilling piercing thunderstorms
and laser alike lancinating lightnings
the celestial symphony of the skies
adding himself to the maddening dance
of all the phantoms gathered in the street
the phantoms of the night, phantoms of the dance
phantoms of the ghost, of love, of heart
of desire even, phantoms of life
whatever other phantoms larger than life
He, the poet became himself a phantom
dancing maddeningly in his apartment
till he collapsed and has fallen down onto the floor
his silhouette reflected for a moment
in the skyline of the New York City's skies
and accentuated as much by a new celestial lightning

Oh, you the true poet, the poet of New York City
reach for a pen, your scintillating wand
and a starlit star—ship capable to travel
across vast universes upon universes
and the inner worlds where our souls stay
Change this world, dear poet of New York City
for a better one, more human, cherishing freedoms
May the celestial symphony adds music of liberation
to all your efforts, my dear poet of New York

XLVI

WHERE THE LIGHT OF SHADOWS FALL

Oh, phantoms, phantoms, my beloved phantoms

phantoms of the Universe and phantoms of this Earth

phantoms of the Day and of the Night

phantoms of poetry, of arts, of creation

phantoms of love, of desire, of heart

Inspire this poet, bring him to the tops

of his creative skills and let him create

amaranthine masterpiece of sparkling poetry

bring then this on the tray before the very God

Appease Him. No more Wrath of God!!

Children of Universe

A handsome man with a blond shag and a hat in his hands
knelt in a chapel alongside a busy highway
He looked at enormous image of the Holly Virgin
and having her as a witness he prayed aloud
fervently, with dampened eyes and a drop of tear
expressing his utmost love to a woman he seemed to have lost
Images of all the good times he had with her
swirled through his mind like fast moving winds

' I am your hunter of stars, no red lights can stop me
a hunter catching most beautiful, youthful stars
and placing them on a starry necklace, a symbol of love
to shine on your neck looking like that of a ballet swan
a necklace with the emerald alike sparkling cosmic rays
being a symphony of all love we have expressed so far
a theatrical play Romeo and Juliet alike, full of drama
a heavenly comedy as much, with plentiful of carefree laugh

You are my virgin of all times I am falling for
rising like a phoenix any time I think of you
towards the Nevada skies high above the Silver State
disappearing then somewhere there among stars

XLVIII

WHERE THE LIGHT OF SHADOWS FALL

I am a hunter of stars indeed, my darling, raging on fire
and I shall find you one day and won't let you go
even if I had to fly through the fiery starry balls
and into the abyss alike Black Hole, risking entrapment

We are children of the Universe, you and me, forever
you a woman, me a man, longing to each other
Perhaps you are gone for now, you my Big Bang
but I don't believe a second you won't come back
and I shall see you back coming to me with a lightning
cos we are destined to each other, sooner or later
I believe it and I pray for it, here in this Chapel of God
here, before Face of Our Lady, the most holly of all

It is a quiet calm after the thunderstorm right now
and only rain is sipping still, sounding a beat of music
to the Beethoven's Appassionata in Ohio skies
and I was just dancing in the rain knowing you shall watch
before I came into this Chapel of God to pray
No, there shall never be rivers in the wasteland
but phosphorescent harvest for both of us
cos we are children of Universe in the glory of love

Yes, I am a hunter of the stars for you, my darling
on my star-ship to the very ends of the Universe
seeking you till I shall find you, with a thunder

XLIX

gifting you with a necklace and rings of stars, diamond alike
letting the nights and days roll like in a ballet musical
The Phantoms of the Ghost shall return to their caves, indeed
Oh, hallelujah, hallelujah, sing the chorus of angels
sing the elegy of a man loving a woman most dear to his
heart !!

I am your painter and a photographer with a silver beard
portraying all your angelic charms with my heart
as if you were a woman with a harp and a trumpet in your hand
a violin, a saxophone and a synthesizer at your side
sending sweetest ever music of angelic dimensions
through the masterful 3D canvas of the sky
and catching on the way all the sensual tastes of any
witnesses
sending us plentiful kisses and wishes of the best

Come, come back to me, shine like angel you are
shatter me, put me on fire, let me dance the way you love
cos we are really destined to each other, a ballet of love
and you shall realize it sooner or later, our ballet of life
You had ascended thunderously like a fiery phoenix
and you shall descend triumphantly like a phoenix
Together again for all times to come, my darling
cos we are children of Universe, united in sweet love '

WHERE THE LIGHT OF SHADOWS FALL

A tear dropped yet again from his dampened eyes
which he closed momentarily to suppress his emotions
He felt someone came up and knelt next to him
It felt as if a whirlwind of mysterious air danced a tango
the tango of love he used to dance with the woman he loved
He opened his eyes and could not believe what he saw
his beloved woman alike Holly Virgin was kneeling side by side
and looked at him lovingly, knowing she came home

They kissed passionately each other in a way lovers do
said farewell to Saint Mary in the chapel, the holiest of all
and holding each other heartily entwined in their arms
went outside to a red colored, fiery Lamborghini
They got in and drove up the highway towards Rocky
Mountains and the Colorado skies embracing the mountains
They, the hunters of stars, woven of their love
They, the children of Universe, finally united in love
This time there was a snowy, wintry scenery on the way
Wherever they looked they saw welcoming arms of lady the
winter which finally descended upon the Earth like a fully
snowy phoenix.

Symphony of Stars

Symphony of Stars

greatest orchestra of the Universe

Alpha and Omega

all galactics participating

all star–ships

Lovers dancing

in the winds of interstellar dust

sparkling stars sending rays

in their cobwebs

enabling lovers to move on

Stellar harps and violins

synthesizers and saxophones

pianos and whatever other musical instruments

built of the stars' rays

are playing music of the stars

Symphony of Stars

goes on and on

Angels are dancing

cosmic adventurers are dancing

the whole Universe is dancing

You're welcome, people of Earth

to join this music of the stars

WHERE THE LIGHT OF SHADOWS FALL

Come on, sing and dance

make your day and your night

fill your lives with a joy

Look upon the stars whoever you are

see the Symphony of the Stars

all their rays joining together

in spectacular outbursts

the music of all times

Symphony of Stars

amaranthine music of the stars

lovers in arms

heartbeat of music of all times

Oh, go on, Symphony of Stars!

Symphony of Sky and Earth

Look at the pulsating rings

around the Sun

whose beams of its rays

spread

into the celestial blue sky

with a mastery

of an orchestra of all times

Heavenly one

addressed to human kind

It's obvious invitation

to have a party

What a symphony it is

one of the Heavens and Earth

the trumpets of the skies

and their harps, and violins

Earth's saxophones

Dj's vibrating rhythms of music

all supported by dancers

ready to have their party

all the day and all the night

Look, the party began

celestial fireworks of music

in the very bright day

But there are though shadows

dark ones

not wanting to disappear

Although the rays are bright

although flowers flourish

the leaves of the trees dance

adding nicely to the music

demons are though dancing

in the darknesses

of the guilty minds

Just look at the sin city

the sin states

Earth engulfed by sin

Like twilights upon twilights

like some strangest creatures

unearthly

perhaps even devils

from the deepest abysses

of guilty minds

stony hearts

This darknesses

as if forces of darkness

beam back

from time to time

trying to destroy

overwhelming wish

for lights of progress

Yet the cobwebs of the Sun's rays

beam at us stronger and stronger

washing us from our sins

and giving us hope

Are we ready to stand up

to the challenges ?

Wash our sins from us

as Jesus Christ did it to Saint Jan ?

Let us begin new chapters

of our lives

put them on track

from the very beginning yet again

We have though learned !!

Look at the skies now and at our Earth

Goodness is emerging victorious

throwing demons back to abyss

locking them there

and never letting them out again

What happens now

is a tribute

to the symphony of the skies

the orchestra of the Sun's rays

the philharmonic of the stars yet to come

dancing angels of the day and the night

A haunting celebration

of love taking the world by storm

The party has really began

joys of love, joys of life

joining the symphony

of the skies and Earth for good

Threads of Love

Stars in all their dimensions

universes upon universes

celestial angels in arms

symphonies of the skies

the Earth itself embraced

by the Heavens as they are

and two of us on an island

the island of love, our love

resembling Crusoe's fabled isle

somehow a celestial star in itself

as looked upon from a distant space

Oh, angels, angels, angels

play us music of love

play on your violins and harps

on your trumpets, synthesizers

Sing us, angels, oh angels

songs sweetest to our ears

and dance us, oh angels

dance us a dance full of love

the whole day and whole night

till the very morning of dawn

then twilight and life giving sunrise

Perhaps the stars are in their trillions

perhaps universes are upon universes

angels in arms in their paradises

Heavens in everlasting peace

things happening in dual worlds

but we, the two deep rooted lovers

stay embraced in our arms

listening to music from the Sun

and music of the distant stars

forever loving each other

and never intending to leave

'cause this would be abomination

if we did

Oh, angels, angels, angels

spread your wings wide

and fly down to our island

the island of love only

See us loving each other

and dancing to the tunes

of the breezes of the wind

of morning's tiny drops of water

falling from the leaves of wild flowers

of the Sun's harp

with it's strings

purely of the Sun's rays

Form then a ring around us

and dance together with us, oh angels

We're two people in love
Don't ask how old we are
don't ask who we are
what we do
what are our preferences
our likes and dislikes
our dreams and desires
our passions
and what brought us
to this island of nature's splendor
our amaranthine island of love
Don't ask all those questions
'cause love has only one name
one and only one, just love
Oh, angels, angels, angels
scintillating angels of the day
and twinkling angels of the night
angels of love, of desires
of everlasting life, of joy
let's really enjoy our love
without looking at the passing time
Just look up the sky
and see world's greatest orchestra
the vibrating rays of the Sun
giving way to the rays of the stars
and ending in our kisses

WHERE THE LIGHT OF SHADOWS FALL

the kisses of love, sweet love

The power of our love

is stronger than gravest storms

No one shall ever be able

to split us, one from another

no passing time either

nor even the witch death with a scythe

no unfriendly strangers

old ladies spreading lies

We all know everything in our lives

is passing away sooner or later

Our lives are passing

time is passing

Yet our love shall remain

for all times to come

'cause love is borderless, even in time ...

Oh, angels, angels, angels

play your celestial symphony

more spectacular

than Broadway musicals

than rock on Wembley

Sensation White in Arena

Play us angels, oh angels

sing and dance us, oh angels

May we feel ourselves

like royals of love in the stars

having everything we wish

May joy of our love

and joy of our life

transcends into hearts

of every human being across the world

Oh, join us all, oh angels

and let's drink the elixirs of love

royal everlasting love.

Linde

Griffis

Thin Ice

Walking on thin ice is what we're doing

One fragile step at a time

Giving ourselves a little more

With each step we take

As each one is cautiously taken

Will this be the step that shatters and breaks

Or will the ice thicken and hold the weight?

Walking on thin ice is what we're doing

In hopes true love we will find

Believing the ice will thicken and hold strong

Through the test of time.

Deep Waters

God is moving although it may seem

That at times He is not doing a single thing!

The waters are too deep

Or so we think

For us to ever recuperate.

Our God is too big to not move at all,

No matter the struggle

He will not let us fall.

Those waters may seem too deep to swim

But God's got our hand.

He won't let us sink

But swim.

Grace

The grace that comes to this race

What has been will be

From here to the end of eternity

No matter what it is that may be

It won't make a difference once we can all see

To many lives that have been lost

Too much for too high a cost

Our lives have been twisted

Too many to be listed

What is life without passion and love

It's lost when we doubt the above

Come to the grace

Live life at your own pace

It's time to rise above

Let go

Let your passion show

Allow yourself to be true to who that is

You're the best that there is

Give it away and the more you will get

It's not gonna hurt you one little but

Jut allow grave

Don't lose the race

Take a Walk

Come take a walk with me
Skies of blue and fields of green
Let's go somewhere we've never been
Travel far to foreign lands
We will cruise along in the Mercedes Benz
Driving til this land ends
Come let's go and take a flight
In the Learjet all through the night
Come take a walk with me
I'll hold your hand
Well see the greenest of all the land
Bluest oceans we've ever seen
Fly away with me
Not just for this night
Don't ever let this go
Fields of green and mountain snow
Come take a walk with me
Take my hand and never let go.

Chains

The chains are too tight

There will be no breath tonight

These clouds of darkness consume me

Leaving its grip on my destiny

So much life had been wasted

Nothing left to be tasted

Bitterness has taken its grip

So tight to think it might slip

Into the vast nothingness of what has become

Death is but a blessing left undone

Can you feel the gravity pulling you down

Aching for you to wear this dark crown

Into the darkness of this night

You never know why your filled with fright

The sobering fact of tomorrow's remorse

Will leave you trembling on the course

To keep the chains from pulling you down

You take a step but lose the crown

The depths of this angst will kill you yet

What brought you here don't forget

Troubles that started long ago

Have fiercely taken their control
One simple thing will shake this fear
Letting go and allowing God to appear

Lust and Love

Lust can leave you shamed and bleeding on the floor.

It's grip is something that can't be ignored.

Never really knowing that you deserve more.

Leaving you crumbled and shattered to the core.

Love will take you gently by the hand.

It sensation will never leave the land.

Such magnificent electricity growing stronger with each wave
of ecstasy.

It's the way you feel this day, growing stronger along the way.

Love encompasses your all, it will never allow you to fall.

It will never leave you in that heap on the floor, it gently carries
you through the door.

It wraps it arms around you with gentle strength, allowing you
to be more complete.

Love never fails, it's always true.

Love will never leave you!

To Live a Life

To live a life of pure contentment
What would that be
As we live in a world of such depravity.
Just look around and you will see
That we are nowhere close to where we should be
Parents are fighting
While their children are starving.
We cater to our addictions
While ignoring our afflictions.
We look down our noses
At those who oppose us.
To live a life of pure contentment
What would that be
As we live in a world of such depravity.

Alone

As I sit alone in here
I think about the ones so near
Those that knew me oh so well
Those that thought we'd all go to hell
In no way did I fear
That one day
They would all disappear.

Alyson

Rewick

JUNE

On that June evening in Montgomery,

You flashed a grin and kissed my hand

And I was yours

The night was burgeoning with life and sound and fragrance

The primroses were still green, but you picked one for me

And tucked it behind my ear

Oh, I remember those nights

The humid evenings by the shadowed lawns

And the picnics by the mansion

I laughed at everything you said

And you called me lovely, princess, dearest

I fell and tumbled through the summer

Into your sheltering arms

I did not fear the cooling winds of autumn

As you held me

In our summer, our youth

And though June has faded

My love has not.

Returning Hope

A wordless hope stirs

As I dream of halcyon days

And powder–blue skies.

The air is thick and sweet,

Redolent of lilacs,

And the lawn is shaded

By all the greenery of June.

The ides of March is over

And Caesar slain,

But there is hope in the temperate winds of May.

April is the passageway,

The transitioning, the golden month.

It forms a daisy bridge between frigid winter

And burgeoning Spring, giving life

And hope to stagnant hearts

ON A NIGHT IN FEBRUARY

I reach to you across the night

Scattering snow with my fingertips

As I pass the frosty stars

And traverse the stretch of blue

Midnight rustles her skirts

And cloaks the frigid world

Still, I find you

In the ivory shadows

Regal upon a snow bank,

My Winter Prince

We pause, and the stars circle us

Like fireflies,

  Illuminating our faces

As we join our lips

And melt

Resistance

I can feel the world changing again

The slate grey sky is heavy and the world is trembling,

trembling

A leaf is loosed from its branch, brittle,

Straining against the wind

And it dances and twists

And then drifts, giving no resistance

To the cold fingers of monolithic autumn.

The world is changing, so I sigh

And dive into the wind.

A View of Earth From Space

Tell me, have you seen

the earth blossom before you

a vibrant jewel against the dark of space

Have you felt the cavernous silence of the abyss

the loneliness, the hollow hum,

the insignificance of all of this

Have you floated above, have you fallen

through the atmosphere of an unmarked world

a tabula rasa, an echo chamber

so far from the place we called home

This is it, the future

a world of sterility and isolation,

and potential, and worlds unknown.

This is our corner of the universe,

Pulsating, waiting

For the next big bang.

This is it–

This is

Home.

Just

I am just

Someone, human

Unjust

That I should limit myself with words,

Labels and definitions

When the fluidity of being

Is contained in the lexicon, the vernacular

The green chat bubble of an IMessage.

"I am" has no meaning,

And my face is a collection of pixels,

My name a few kilobytes of information

In a Google cache

I am no one, I am just

Me, but the digital footprints follow

And our lives are indexed in the Cloud

An Effluence of Words

Turn the spigot, turn,

I want to speak

But my mouth is arid

And your stare is acrid.

"Speak," you dare me,

"Make a mistake,"

And I clamp my mouth shut,

Closing it over the songs, the dreams,

The screams, the complaints,

The essence of being and the terror of –

Not, but the silence,

The silence is key.

I have no voice, no place,

I did not exist, I cannot exist

And you laugh at me with that wry, wan smirk,

Sickly and sneering, mockingly defiant,

But I take a breath

And part my lips to exhale,

And my tongue is loosened

By an effluence of words.

A Butterfly in May

May I be as free as the black–winged butterfly,

Silk in the sun and blue in the shade?

May I tremble, may I flutter,

May I tumble on the wind,

Ignorant of the world

And held captive only by the sky?

May I soar and soar

Until my antennae are tangled

With wisps of cloud,

Cirrus and cumulus

Veiling my compound eyes?

May I fall at the end of my days

To the welcoming bed of a rose petal,

Folded in exhaustion, frail and brittle,

May I do it all?

An Elegy for New York

I see a vacant skyline

And all I can think of

Is what used to be

And what could have been.

Castor and Pollux raced to the stars

And stopped a few feet short of heaven.

Scintillating and sharp,

They stood two decades strong

On top of the city,

the world.

And now, what is left?

Hope, perhaps

But above all

Resilience.

August's Defiance

I can recall an evening

When the moon was wreathed by clouds

The cricket's song was waning

But the August wind was loud.

It rushed across the treetops

And in between the stars

Crying, "Please, do not forget me!"

To the Pleiades and Mars.

There was a strong consensus

On that summer night

"Autumn might be on its way

But we'll put up a fight!"

Rose

Mary

McKenzie

BATTLE

There is a battle for my mind

The good the bad are intertwined

Sometimes I do protest

I know which is best

Go away, do not molest

There is a battle for my mind

Sometime I'm feel fine

I feel I'm running out of time

My mountain is to hard to climb

There is a battle for my mind

I have lost my youth, not in my prime

I was young, now I am old

Seems like everything is out of control

There is a battle for my heart and soul

There is a battle for my mind

I need   solace, I need time

Will you walk with me?

Hold my hand, help me   stand

Help me walk on solid ground, not sinking sand

There is a battle for my mind
I want to go home, not left behind
I feel dazed and so confused
I feel unloved, I feel used
I've live my life, I've paid my dues

There is a battle for my mind
Can't move, I'm in a bind
I cannot see, I am so blind
My heart, my spirit I cannot find
There is a battle for my mind

BABY

BABY

In the dark you cried

No place to run and hide

Life taken away from you

No liberty, or happiness to pursue

Baby, what evil did you do

Sacrificed on the abortion alter

No time for you,

Lamb to the slaughter

Just another inconvenience in the way

She who should protect wanted to play

Baby wanted to live, you had no say

I will fight for your right to live

My life if I need to would give

Baby the most innocent of all

You are God's little one if I recall

Baby on the alter, so sweet and small

Baby my heart hurts, you never had a chance

Going to parties, school, or have romance

To be a Mom or a Dad,

A chance you've never had

WHERE THE LIGHT OF SHADOWS FALL

Baby I am so hurt and profoundly sad

Your Father has gathered you home

Baby you'll never be all alone

Your cries in the night now gone

Happy and playing around God's Thorn

You joined the angels, singing a new song

Baby, dear baby, you have come home.

Scottish Prince

I loved you for a very long time

this Scottish prince of mine

I look into brown eyes

and loose myself in them

What wonders await

yet I know our fate

I would take you away

to highland and glen

And love you always

not caring my sin

I would go with you

never turning back

I will give you my love

and   nothing you'd lack

having you   so far way

but it still reaches me

and we say what we may

One day I will find you

on that far away shore

I will have you for ever more

speak to me in your Gaelic tongue

LXXXIX

WHERE THE LIGHT OF SHADOWS FALL

melting my heart like snow in the warm sun

I am yours and you are mine

we are together till the end of time...

Clans

Aye, the Campbell's

and the McKenzie's

were a warring clan

taking from each other

what ever they would demand

They fought bloody battles

the ax and swords did wield

Neither would give in

until the last one killed

This lasted over many years

there was loss, pain and tears

The Chieftain Clan leaders

would not budge or move

Till they sought new ways

to their anger then to sooth

Aye, it took years, and days

to bring them the Clans peace

They walk now together

their warring days have ceased

Over the Scottish highlands

their history of which they speak

Their   Gaelic tongue makes a song

of triumph, and sweet relief..

Aye the Campbell's

and the Mckenzie's

are as united as can be

Until I being a Campbell

married a McKenzie...

Grandma's Love

Grandma sat with her hands folded

sitting in her favorite rocking chair

Looking out the window at the snow

Falling from heaven to the earth below

The room was quiet now, no voices to hear

Her family gone but they would come again next year

the dinner, the gifts that made her shed a tear

She reminisced lovingly of bye gone years

when he children were little, they were so dear

her children now have babies she loves as much

playing with the little one, the babies dimples to touch

Putting away dishes, and some food she prepared

not much left, giving the rest to the children to share

Going back to look at her chair, she spotted a gift

Just waiting for her twinkling eyes to see

Smiling and opening it quickly, she thought, for me?

Inside she saw a treasure and a sweet note

from her youngest granddaughter a box of tea

This is for you Gram for a cold winters night

It will keep you warm till I can hold you tight

She wondered how much more she could love

Knowing this special love came only from above

then gazing fondly at the beautiful star

Nestled on the top of the decorated tree

I love my family, just like Christ loves me

Her family would come again next year

Her heart was full, happy as could be

Knowing all good things will come

To all Granny's if you only believe

thanking God for my family

Country Love

I saw this boy

This country boy

The sun shone in his smile

I walked his country mile

Oh, my heart fell at his feet

His sweetness to seek

He was shy

This country guy

I wanted to know him more

I feel hard, he rocked me to my core

This country boy

I took a chance

Old fashion romance

I took his hand

I walked on his country land

This country man

I stayed with him for a while

Basking in the sun of his smile

I held him so tenderly

WHERE THE LIGHT OF SHADOWS FALL

Loving, my country boy and me

Time passed, I could not stay
I had to go on my way
Going back in time
When he shined
This county boy of mine

I once was young
We had our fun
We left nothing undone
Me and my country son

I was bold
Now I am old
He still thinks of me, I am told
He will never be old

I have no regrets
This country man I met
I live in memories
He was a blessing from above
This my boy, my man
This my country love.

WE WERE SO VERY YOUNG

My thoughts are going way back when we first met

our first time away from home

So excited we said to be on our own

We were so very young

We met at bible school, learning the golden rule

we needed this in our live, it was our Godly tool

I wanted to follow our Lord and so did you

singing, we'll go where you want us to go dear Lord

we'll be what you want us to be, on land or on the sea's

We were so very young

We married after graduation, ready to meet the world

then we had our babies, a little boy and girl

Life was very hard we soon began to see

We were so very young, you and me

Our lives went on, day after day

we raised our two, just me and you

We were so very young

Then as life goes, it got harder by the day

it wasn't easy and one day you went away

We were so very young

John, you went home to be with our Lord

your work on Earth was done

But we will always remember you,

your wife, your Daughter and your Son

In 7 years years we lived our live in the Son

John, we were so very young.

The Grave

I stood on the thresh hold of the grave

Jump, jump in, I heard the dark man say

The winds blew the dogs barked and howled

The very trees had demonic creepy scowl

I wasn't sure what I wanted to now to do

But take away the pain that's all I knew

I looked in to the deep dark cold abyss

The curled snakes gave sneering hissed

It seemed my destiny had come at last

In that moment, was my future and past

Then as I compelled and heeded the call to jump in

I screamed ,try just one more time and begin again

As I pondered what to do, I saw him standing

I could see evil in him through and through

I shuddered and I quaked, I had a decision to make

Not this time in my life..I want to live for heavens sake

Stepping back for the grave, I turned away and heard him

say

Go, go away, it's not time for you to die tonight or this day

My heart pounded and beat, I turned, I ran, I stumbled, I

fell

I was gaining ground I started to moan and cry, then I

sailed

I flew through the trees so high, I even touch the dark

night sky

Yes, I would stay alive, I wouldn't die, it would work if I

tried

I came to land where I did live..I would sale all I owned

Just to be happy in my own humble home

I forgot about that one dark cold night,

Then...I saw him again...this is not right

Didn't he say I was Ok, time for me to live another day

Oh yes he said, I spoke true, now..it tonight, and I've

come for you

So never want to end your life, don't even think it is my

advice

It is not yours to take, not yous to make, so think once or

twice

Or this could be your last day and certainly your last

night..

I Remember

I lost you 44 years ago

It tore out my heart and soul

I came home and found you

Your death was seemed untrue

We had two little ones

So I knew I had to go on

Making a life for us three

It was so difficult for me

I left you and moved away

Not knowing what to do or say

I took our babies to a new home

It was difficult to leave you alone

But I did, and life had it's storms

You would be so very   proud

They have with families God allowed

But the legacy followed us

Sharon lost her Roy, we were crushed

They had three little children

Now she had to begin   again.

How could this happen one more time

I didn't want to believe, it pained my mind

Then, the Lord gave me a second chance

I found love and a new romance

We had a daughter Steve and I

Oh dear Lord, then her husband died

She had three to look out for

But she was up to the chore

She handled it and loved once more

Marrying a wonderful man James

And with her new family she moved south

Mom and daughters losing a spouse

How can this be, what are the odds

I've never understood, so much pain it caused

I do know one thing to be true

God has a plan for me and you

Keep the faith, our trials will soon be over We will know

the why's, for two daughters and their Mother.

Empty Rooms

The house is cold and bare

I look but no one is there

Darkness is all I see

Where once was you and me

Rooms empty, full of   hollow sounds

I open the door, memories scattered around

Pain in every nook, closet and corner

A home where love has gone, with no honor

I stumble through the rooms

Emptiness fells it   like a tomb

My tears run down my weathered face

Every where I look, I see your trace

My feet take me to our room

Love was happy, like a rose in bloom

It is now gone, all to painfully soon

Our sun does not give light, only gray of the moon

I take one last dreadful look

Reading the last chapter in our book

Was it you, was it I, that love forsook
Crying, sobbing, my body shook..

I turn and walk out the door
Pain to great, can't take any more
Following the path and out the gate
God!!! help me, hear me for heaven sake!

I stop, I take my last fleeting glance
Thinking maybe there is one more chance
No..there is no heart, no love, no romance

I am hollow like our home
No spirit, no soul, no marrow in my bones
I am done, all hopes   diminished
I am dying, my life is now finished..

Who I am..

I've grown to like who I am
Doesn't depend on woman or man
It took so long to understand
I am fine the way I am

Try not to change who you are
We are much better by far
Reaching out for our   own star

When I was little, and so very young
I didn't fit in, no song I   sung
I was so sad most of my life
Unhappy, so full of dread and strife

As I've grown and I have aged
I am so thankful, I have sagged
Took years, took   so long
Finding where I Belonged

So let me tell you while I may
Say what you mean, and mean what you say

You will misstep, and fall along the way

But, oh you will sparkle brightly one day

God made us who we are suppose to be

I'm not like you, your not like me

Let's shine our light for all the world to see

Growing in grace for all eternity

Then you will say to all you can

I've grown to like who I am

It doesn't depend on woman or man

I'm fine the way I AM...

I never knew a Father's love

When I was just a child

I always felt so different

truth, he never wanted me

I could plainly see

I went to school

others laughed

A little girl didn't know

why they were being

so cruel

I asked my Mom,

why it was this way

She looked at me

so much pain and hurt on her face

She cried, she didn't know what to say

I always felt I should not have been born

to sleep the night or to see the early morn

I once heard, your heart can't be at peace

until you find all the pieces

This is so true for me to say

So till then, I will be content

I will   love my Daddy from far away

I will always have you in my heart

I now hope will can see

from Heaven home

and you will love me

I love you Daddy..

MAMA

Mama, we started out, just you and me Daddy wasn't a
part of our lives and this was so sad to see
Our first home was Grandpa's old car which didn't get us
very far
A migrant work camp in the grape fields of the south
was our humble beginnings and we lived from hand to
mouth

I never knew how it was to be fully fed ,
my belly was empty and sometimes I was so scared
You worked so hard to keep me by your side It was hard,
we suffered,
you told me the truth about truth about our lives and you
never lied

We worked together, side by side you and I
cotton,plums, grapes, potato's and cherries
It was hot, and back breaking work, but we survived

I didn't know what it was to have a normal child hood
but I loved you Mama, you taught me well, and I
understood

When my Brothers and Sisters came to our family, what a
gift they were to me,
I loved them like my own Ma, they made me so happy!

Mama, you loved all of your kids, one no better then the
other
You filled our lives with compassion, prayers, and love
and how we loved you, our hearts were blessed with you
Mother

Thank you Mama for all you've done for them and me
When I was little, I dreamed of being a Mama just like you
You were the example of a Mom, the kind I wanted to be

Mama, you have been in Heaven for almost 15 years
we've had our share of loneliness and cried many tears.
But until we meet again some happy and glorious day
we will hold you in our hearts until we can hold you in our
arms

God keep you Mama, so wait for us up there,
we we'll sit around the supper table, safe from our worldly

care.

I reach out you in my humble prayer, wait for us Mama, we

will so be there..

Covered

Cover me deep so that I may sleep

Under a bed of clay

no more to awake

No breaths to take

with sorrow from within

My pain is strong, my song is gone

I shall not rise again

So cover me deep so that I may sleep

Under a bed of clay

My soul takes wing

peace may it bring

so I may have my song again

It carries me away to a better day

Into the sky of blue

and my heart is renewed

So till then I say to you

Cover me deep so that I may sleep

Under a bed of clay

Ryan

Christiano

'Love Letter'

My Dearest One,

I saw you with him in the park today
Your hand clasped in his like ours used to be

Memories like leaves scattered by autumn wind.

I read today you are to wed him
In the chapel beside the brook
Where we first embraced

Left with the whisper of what could have been

I saw you in the park today
Hand in hand with a little girl
An angel who was your reflection
It broke my heart and shattered my soul

Shards of glass that can't be unbroken

I wish you only happiness
It's as if we never met

That's just as well

These words are my farewell

The words of this unsent letter

Left dampened by tears

'Depthless Darkness'

Feet upon the softly fallen snow
Looking down the depthless darkness
Mirror beneath of still and blackened glass
Beckoning, taunting, calling
The snow falls softly upon the path

Toes touching cold concrete
Moonlight the mistress of this night
The snow falls softly upon the path

The wind stills its dance
Silence shares its secret
The depthless darkness calls us all
The snow falls softly upon the path

Distant lights blink their distress
The time has come for eternal rest
Arms grasp the air
One last whispered prayer
The depthless darkness rushes forth
The snow falls softly upon the path

WHERE THE LIGHT OF SHADOWS FALL

Hope still shimmers in the fading light

A faltering flame

This night

The promise of a renewed twilight

The snow falls softly upon the path

'Waking Dreams'

How did I get here
Defined by my fears
When all my hopes
Gave way to tears

You say nothing is wrong
But you're a melody without song
How long
Must light yield to night
How long
Must dreams give way to
Life

Illusions of youth
Fade away
Life is fleeting
In the vanishing season

You are the flower
That flourishes
In the moonlit hour

WHERE THE LIGHT OF SHADOWS FALL

The rose that grows

In the glistening snow

Does not know

Why beauty flows

The robin that cries

In winter skies

Knows not why

Beauty thrives

Echoes may fade away

The sun may set each day

But your beauty remains unchanged

This truth sees me through

To loving you

The beautiful dreamer

Who laughed and danced

In a field of stars

The beautiful dreamer

Whose twilight eyes mesmerize

Those dreams may seem

To scatter

As ripples upon a pond

But they go on

WHERE THE LIGHT OF SHADOWS FALL

In rhythm to every beat of your heart
They are never gone

Dream in the waking hours
Then you have power
Over the doubters
Beauty bellows
Eternal night yield to light

Ana

Vargas

The Cake

Loving father,
You knew me since before I was born,
Worked your fingers to the bone

A divine masterpiece you made
With the reddest strawberries and darkest chocolates

This my love, is for you
For your special day, for your celebration
From me to you

Its intoxicating, dizzying aroma
Its blinding beauty, made me do it

Just one taste, one dip of my delicate finger, was not enough,
With both hands full I took what was mine
and betrayed your love,

And with burning tears you looked at me,
Told me you loved me still.

Stone Walls

Stone walls, ancient in their majestic beauty

Standing the test of time

Though anarchy and wreckage have made their mark

They Ivy, resilient in its ways

Manages to creep in still

And in the quiet fragility of peace,

A witness to hope, like a true survivor

Ever resisting, never forgetting

While You Were There II

Lonely nights are forever cold
Forgotten stories never told

While you were there our love grew
Only to be left with a memory of you

Nothing more to do, nothing more to say
I only pray that I wish I could stay

In a place only you and I called our abode
Now I'm left alone with the feelings you arose

I find myself asking how could this be?
Unbelieving we just weren't meant to be

Not knowing how to end the story
Found with love that ended without glory

Unable to let go, forced to let go
Standing alone thinking of how you loved me so

You were drawn to the light that filled me with kindness

WHERE THE LIGHT OF SHADOWS FALL

And like a beggar I followed you into the darkness

Stuck in the line between heaven and hell
Praying like a pagan for you to get well

I am the daughter of light
I'm going home to wait to reunite.

Metanoia

Suffering the death of romance
Her repenting heart takes a chance

The time for asking is consumed
Her crumbling life is resumed

Facing down the truth, tearing down the walls
Of a lovelorn dream out of which she crawls

A woman ever leaning
Now committed to her weaning

No longer afraid of herself
She entertains her name in and of itself

Trusting the one who created trust
To be delivered from this sinful lust

In My Skin

The feel of soft cotton between my fingers
pacifies me from the torment of my passions

The broken record of the rosary plays in my mind
The beating heart of my baby lying next to me
competes for my attention

The eyes of my soul turn to my inward beauty as
The smell of vanilla on my skin reminds me that I'm still alive.

Hello

Kiss my forehead and bless my flight

For your love has been my true delight

The years have fallen by in vain

The loneliness and the waiting game

Were a scourging passion like the Lord's

To live or to love, have never been at odds

So I choose death that I can live to love

I shake the dust from my feet as I fly like a dove

Farewell to 2010

It was the year of our Lord MMX,

Lived to intense proportions,

I laughed till it hurt,

Worked till I bled, and

Cried till death's shadow teased.

Without an ounce of life left for you,

I must bid you adieu:

I am sad to let you go my friend.

I am glad that you are now gone.

Though you will not be missed,

you will not be forgotten.

It has been truly an honor to have enjoyed you

And survived you.

Tears of sorrow have been shed for you.

I now leave you with the clink of a glass for a happy ending.

To a happily ever after!!

Cheers!

My life is a Prayer

I asked for wisdom, that I would not make mistakes,
I was made a fool that I would humbly look to God for
guidance.

I asked for love that I may be happy,
I was given loneliness that I may find fulfillment in God.

I asked for success, that I may impress,
I was made a failure that I would serve God all the days of my
life.

I asked for riches that I may be like the others,
I was given the Eucharist that I may be like Christ.

I asked for justice that I may get my revenge,
I was given mercy that I could be a saint.

I asked to be a great mother,
I was given a great son that I may give my life for him.

I am blessed among women,
For the Lord has done great things for me.

Vanilla Lullaby

If your face were a cake

It would be a vanilla cake

With chocolate m&m eyes

And strawberry lips

I would eat your nose first

Or should I eat it last?

I would take a bite from your chin

And save the rest for another time.

A poem for my son on his birthday.

Joy

Blevins

'Reality Check'

I sit here and wonder why

Things have to end the way they do.

As each day passes ...
It doesn't get easier
As all my thoughts keep
turning to you.

I Love you, I Miss you
I wish you were here
To wipe away every tear and
put at ease my greatest fear.

Your Laughter, Your Smile
is in my heart
Which helps me to ease
the hurt I felt
When God decided it was
your time to part.

WHERE THE LIGHT OF SHADOWS FALL

So now your gone

and I sit all alone

Reminiscing thru memories

Trying to find the reality that you left behind.

'Night Terrors'

The black of night it tries to seize
The blowing winds whispers
through the trees
Dark holds a secret so scary and rare
One of which it refuses to share

Shadows try keeping low to the ground
Yet falling they make the slightest of sound
Evil reminds us of what the night does hold
And now it's destiny has begun to unfold

Eventually the sun turns night to ash
Its warmth and peace shines through the glass
Even though it radiates so bright and clear
There is still too much to fear

'Lost'

Your life is a mess
and we both know why
yet all you keep saying is
"Just one more high"

I've watched from a distance
when you've gone without
I've heard the rage
that you scream and shout

I've watched you get clean
you're so down and depressed
all the while complaining
your life's just not blessed

STOP!

Look in the mirror
look long and hard
is this the way you're choosing
to play your last card?

Rock bottom is where you are living now
do something...cry out...
some way or somehow

Because rock bottom is where
this drug called meth
will leave you to take your very last breath

'Best Friends

I thought you ware my friend
just there to help me through
while I watched her weak and sick
from all the chemo she had to do

Yes you showed me how
to live without pain
so I wouldn't have to deal
when her health didn't regain

You stopped me from the hurt
with continued lie after lie
even helped me not to cope
with why it was her turn to die

I thought I was strong
I thought I was smart
all the while thanking you
for numbing my heart

By the time all was done
it was already too late

WHERE THE LIGHT OF SHADOWS FALL

you had grabbed onto me
but not showed me my fate

You swooped a big bow
and stared at my face
looked me straight in the eyes
then put me in my place

"You see when it comes
to affairs of the heart
I will   stay by your side
we'll never ever part"

"So thank you for trusting me
to help you get through
Once I   knew you were hooked
I sunk my claws into you"

'The Prayer'

What to do
where to start
will God understand
and enter my heart?

Will He help me past
what is to come
or side with the others
and say "I am done"

All I can do is drop to my knees
ask for His mercy
and beg him please
help carry me through
all that I have left to do

Dear God, just help me
find my way back
to the life I once had
but now seem to lack

WHERE THE LIGHT OF SHADOWS FALL

Show me how to live
so simple and carefree
as that is where I am
yearning to be

~Amen~

Ken

Blick

We the Poets

In the beginning there was nothing.

The spirit that imbued the old constitution

gave way to a new resolution.

Where there was nothing; growth appeared.

Words formed that drew us near.

KWB

Some came with fear and doubt of self worth

Much to my disbelief all my grief vanished

A loving family I found inside all with hearts of pure gold

We all have stories to be told.

TKH

Every where we were lead to steer

All we saw was nothing but tears.

Frowning faces wanting a reason to smile

Knowing there was someone to go the extra mile.

Turning a frown upside down

Knowing the Lord would touch this ground.

EDV

WHERE THE LIGHT OF SHADOWS FALL

As we walk hand and hand
creating our poetry
forming our words pen with pen
our love to each other we will send
we are family as you know
and together we all will grow
RMM

Looking forward not turning back
We learned to love each other.
Finding places in the heart
of friendships we discovered.
Time and space will soon now tell
What writings we've uncovered.
NNF

You carry our burdens
and delight in our joys
You help us make music
when we hear only noise
You help us make sense of the tempest inside
In this circle of poets, there's no need to hide
AHR

Rivers of rhyme flow through time
Poetic peaks we seek to climb

WHERE THE LIGHT OF SHADOWS FALL

From seasons of sadness and sorrow
Emerged a better tomorrow

We see our dreams in sight
Beneath the starry moonlit night
As our souls take flight
Our hearts soar to heavenly heights
May this place of poems
Be our eternal home
RPC

A Poetry Alliance Collective

The Phoenix

Fairies flew around my head,
and Dragons perched upon my bed.
The Elve's bridled a uni–corn,
for my daily ride in the early morn.

.

I floated up into the sky,
and looked down from way up high.
I saw a river, perhaps a stream,
shimmering up just like a dream.

.

I plunged into it's murky depth,
and swam upon the eddy's met.
The fear of what was in the sea,
only seemed to heighten me.

.

When I was tired, I took a ride,
upon a 4–wheeler on a mountain side.
With cliffs all around, and wind in my face,
I squeezed the throttle and started to race.

.

But I saw the birds and wanted to fly,
so I sprouted wings and gave it a try.

WHERE THE LIGHT OF SHADOWS FALL

I glided on currents high above earth,
and remembered the times when I had no worth.

.

Pain erupted from deep inside,
and fire flew out from within my eye's.
I scorched the land, I also tore,
and in a blaze, I was no more.

.

And in the ashes, there was bore,
the one who would write to tell the lore.
The master of dreams, the user of diction,
the wizard of words, the dreamer of fiction.

Comfort

Whenever darkness falls,

I struggle to find the peace.

For I know that God is good,

and he want's my pain released.

For in this hour of darkness,

it's hard to see what's right.

It take's a lot of focus,

to finally see the light.

My anger now extinguished,

and in his hands I lay.

I know the pain will go away,

just maybe not today.

For now, I am comforted,

by those I cherish most..,

The Father and the Son,

and of course the Holy Ghost.

May God be with you always,

and light the path you take.

Know that he is with you,

especially when heart's break.

The Wedding Wish

My wish for you today my loves,

as you journey on your way.

May your path be lit by God,

and the devil not lead you astray.

Keep your faith in each other,

even when things go wrong,

for it's because of these trials,

that make a marriage strong.

Hold each other tightly,

and never let go.

because love is like a summers day,

even when there's snow.

Never take advantage,

of the one you hold today.

For what God has given you,

he will someday call away.

So build a life together,

one that's very long.

One that brings you happiness,

and is firm and strong.

Always give God grace,

even when you apart.

May peace and love be with you two,

and always fill your heart.

Shine

Shine shine shine,

It's your time to shine.

Open up your heart

because it's time to shine.

I was on a broken path,

living for today.

I had opportunities,

but I threw them all away.

Smoking dope and getting drunk,

that was the life for me.

It wasn't very hard to find,

plenty of company.

I didn't know it.

God had a plan for me.

What others saw as waste,

God saw a light in me.

He sent his angel,

and I beat her down.

She returned to heaven,
but without her crown.

Smoking dope and getting high,
that's the life for me.
Stop wasting your time,
I'm not worth your sympathy.

I don't pray,
I yell when I'm mad.
I raised my fist to Heaven
but I cried out loud.

Shine shine shine,
I wanted to shine.
But I was too deep,
and I was covered in slime.

The clouds turned black
and then it started to rain.
It washed my soul
and erased my shame.

I was on my knees
when the clouds broke free.
Slicing through the darkness

WHERE THE LIGHT OF SHADOWS FALL

was a ray of light on me.

Aglow in the moment,

I broke down and cried.

I opened up my heart

and let my savior inside.

Shine shine shine,

I started to shine.

I noticed a man

that had been hidden inside.

If I could find redemption,

and your story's just like mine.

Don't give up,

God want's you to shine.

Love Eternal

Hope springs eternal inside of my heart,

through these blue eyes you knew it from the start.

It was me.

Oh yes I see.

.

I've let down my walls too many times,

Running away is how I survived.

You see?

Your love frightened me.

.

Blood rushed to my head and I was spinning fast,

I reached out for help and you came out of my past.

That's true.

Baby I loved you.

.

I couldn't believe and thought it was a joke,

Nobody's ever written things like the things you wrote.

So I ran.

I hope you understand?

.

When I didn't see any reply from you,

I felt empty and cried the night through.

WHERE THE LIGHT OF SHADOWS FALL

You were gone.

I had been so wrong.

.

Happiness shines in my life today,

I see your words and they carry me away!

Be with me.

You still have the key.

To Have

To Have

The sun rises.

But, that's not really true.

Because I feel the universe,

revolves around you!

Every minute I'm with you,

I see heaven unfold.

With every beat of my heart,

and every breath in my soul.

Come run way with me,

and we'll leave reality.

We'll build a life together,

and stay for eternity.

You are the one,

oh, can't you see?

Please open your heart

and see that its me.

My Mothers in Heaven

My Mothers not alive, she had to go away.
So, I find it kind of hard, especially on this day.
I know you raised me up to be quite strong,
But I'm crying today, because I miss you Mom.

I'm not trying to guess at Gods great plan,
who am I to even understand?
But I know in my heart everything is alright,
I'll live for that day when I walk toward the light.

A Mother is Love and she touches your soul,
even in death you can still feel that pull.
A Mother will love you no matter the deal,
she sees in your heart and knows what is real.

Although I do miss her, she watches me,
high in the sky with our majesty.
Smiling from her heavenly home,
as I write for her this Mother's Day poem.

You're not alone

When you cast your last believe in some one who let's you
down again,

all you want to do is curl up and die.

You're not alone.

Every smile that you force, your keeping it all inside,

and all you want is to run and hide.

You spread your love like it was on fire,

you're everyone's hope and desire.

But it happened once again.

That's just the way life is.

You live a life of pain,

getting hurt all over again,

how did it come to this?

Once you were a princess on a holiday,

and now here comes the rainy day's,

you wanna give up and run away.

You're not alone.

Oh no, your never truly all alone.

(no way no how)

Every broken heart becomes another piece of the puzzle,

mixed up and distributed all over the World,

again and again.

Uh, huh.

Until you get it right,

there will always be tears in the night.

YOUR.

NOT.

ALONE.

It should never be this way.

You should never feel alone.

Trust in the Lord,

and he will always lead you home.

No, you never have to be alone.

Rose Mary

Ken

Thaddeus

Elluisa

Emerald Green

The sunrise flows over emerald mountain

A breath taking painting of beauty to behold

Colors, pink, yellow, red and luminous gold

They have to be lived,

it cannot simply be told

To walk in the ancient Redwood groves

The time stand still and yet, unfolds

Angels walk in the morning mist On our sleepy brow

They place a kiss Breath the air,

Life is there and clean Walking in heaven

and the world in between

So come go with me, so much to see

God creations for you and me

Take my hand, walk this land

You will never be the same

Souls being healed in His name

Other beauty has never been seen

This glory, that is emerald green

I will go again to my forest so fine

There, I will commune with the divine

In my land, where there is no time..

RMM

A Mother's Son

How do you speak to a Mother's heart
Give he a son that is handsome and smart

A smile to warm your heart, with love at the very start
His eyes so blue   that shine like the sky
Sweetness that can make you smile with a sigh
Heart so full it can make you cry

He was our precious little boy
We were blessed, our hearts   so full of joy
Our family became four
We had all we need, need we ask for more

We watched you grow to be a man
How proud we were when you took a stand
You went into Navy, and away from me you did go'
I missed you terribly, as my love did grow and grow
I think this Mom's heart gave a little each day
I counted the minutes, the hours, the days you were away

Then you came home to had a new life of your own
You married your Jenni, and started your home
So the day went bye, and you had a son

WHERE THE LIGHT OF SHADOWS FALL

Griffin was your pride, of your life'
Your were a family, your son and your wife

One day you will recall this about your son
How the days were full of life and fun
It past in a fleeting moment, these precious days
One year following another, in beautiful haze

If there was one thing I could change
Every thing would remain the same
I would hold you once again
As a baby boy of so many years ago
I would tell time to   go very slow

Son, I love you more then you could know
You are my heart, my life and my soul
I thank God for sending you to me
Giving me a son, I am so very pleased
RMM

A Valentine's Day Poem

If I could see you one more time,
I'd tell you I love you all over again!
I'd tell you how much my heart,
of you, is still a part.
I'd bend down on one knee,
and I'd ask you tenderly...
Please plant a garden,
with me please!
For in our heart's,
we'll plant the seeds.
Then we'd charge up mountains,
and float like bees.
We'd walk in the clouds,
and feel the gentle breeze.

Together you and I,
we'd paint the river's,
and touch the sky.
There's nothing we couldn't do,
but that's...if,
if I could only be with you.

KWB

How To Say Goodbye

I see it is your time to go home
You have left us behind
With all these feeling of love
Hurt and emotions that start to roam

Why you had to leave we will never know
This rips our hearts as the tears that pour
The loneliness overwhelms
Please just remember we love you so.

Sad how our lives can change in a blink of an eye
When do we know it is okay to let go?
Will we ever feel safe again? Is it okay to love?
How do you know when it is time to say good bye?

Letting go of a loved one is so hard
When is it right?
How do you know?
Does it just come to you like throwing ball in a yard?

Time must go on
The emotions are strong

WHERE THE LIGHT OF SHADOWS FALL

But there is nothing left
My daddy is gone.

E.Vargas

Winter Breeze

Listening to the sound of the wind
Watching the tress dance
Looking at the ice glisten on the trees
All from a glance.

Calming movement
Hearing clash clash
Sounds of Winter
As rain falls with a splash.

Frost on the windows
Cold chills down the spine
Winter breeze
Warm night by the fire with some cheese and wine.

Icecicles on the house
Water comes to a freeze
Oh how I love
This winter breeze.

Elluisa

' Carpathian Skies '

The day belonged to the majestic Carpathian mountains
and the marvelous skies embracing them, the Carpathian skies
Mesmerizing and enigmatic beyond anything to say
fabulous to a highest degree, God's phenomenal creation
The skies were azure blue, not one even grey cloud to be seen
This vast ocean of blue expanses was embraced brotherly
by countless symphonic rays from the godlike Sun
Devine music of the skies above the Carpathian mountains
breathtaking, a heavenly music of the Phantom of the Day

I was tramping through mountain ranges the whole day
feeling united with the nature and her godlike proximity
It was a world in itself, a bewildering wilderness of the nature
all those mountain lakes, flowers one could never see
elsewhere
wild animals seen from time to time, even the brown bears
amazing display of the divine Carpathians in all their royal
dominion
From time to time I looked around curiously for something else
something what I heard from the jovial local mountaineers
to whom nothing here was alien, everything in their scriptures

Any time soon I should find a castle hidden in those mountains deep in their shadow, the castle of Dracula Vlad Tepes himself

the enormously blood thirsty king of all vampires in one person

The stories were the prince turned vampire was still present

and active at nights as centuries ago, more so with passing

time

the prince who lost his beloved princes some centuries ago

in suspicious and very gruesome circumstances, which

enraged him

to such a degree he turned into a vampire in a supernatural

way

and ever since then he was on a killing spree, out of a sheer

rage

never to be satisfied enough, falling for fresh blood from virgins

mainly

I have returned to my camping quite late, feeling a bit a colder

air

a starlit night was already fully blown like some angelic beauty

or even like Marilyn Monroe in her dress blown up in the wind

before a crowd of frenzy photographers, dancing like some

devils

luckily without a trace of them here, on the bosom of nature

What a night it promised to be, under the Carpathian skies

with all the luminously shimmering stars on the curtain of

Heavens

in gentle gust of warm winds, wolves and bears hidden from

sight

in the darkness of the quiet night, sometimes perhaps seen

ghostly

With my tent, my table with candles, a small campfire next

What else did I need ? Yes, a woman, a muse of these

mountains !!

I had a delicious late supper on the table which I consumed

like if I were an enormously excessive gourmand

while the small flames of my candles danced in the soft wind

not strong enough to get them snuffed out, a dance of the

flames

I don't know what happened then, there was a momentary

darkness

as if I lost my consciousness or were kept in blackness

The next sequence was simply thrillingly unearthly,

supernatural

there sat both, Satan himself and God Almighty at the table

Satan's eyes showed endless abyss with wild fires

ten thousands more powerful than nuclear explosions

or even Big Bang supernovas at vast galactic spaces

This horror alike abyss must certainly have been the Hell

God's eyes showed the Heavens, of infinite calmness

and infinite spaces of all Universes, known and unknown

though gathered completely within Him, God Almighty

the Creator of all the Universes, of Infinities upon Infinities
Why did he then tolerated Satan, the devil of devils?
Well, perhaps He had His unfathomable design, His plan
– ' You're mine. ' – Satan said wryly to me, aggressively
I felt instantly burning myself madly out of fear of fears
What have I done Satan wanted me? I was a decent person
I've never harmed anyone, never cheated, why then ?

– ' Not in my life ! Never ever !! ' – I suddenly heard a shout
I was stunned but as much God and Satan themselves
An intensive source of light, tennis ball shaped, jumped
out of my chest and bounced onto the table
I realized this neutron alike ball of intensive light
was nothing else as my soul, my beloved soul, my defender !!
– ' You're not to decide this ! ' – Satan reposted angrily
Bundle of hellish fires flushed out of his eyes, nearly catching
my soul
But then unexpectedly he managed to hit my soul
which bounced all the way towards the neighboring mountains
only to be caught by God's invisible strings alike the ones
used by Spiderman and brought back onto the table

– ' Neither you ' – God Almighty said calmly not even looking
at Satan
and extended His hand to my soul. She bounced happily on
God's hand

– ' You think so ?! ' – Satan reposted yet again, but one could

see

he wasn't so sure of himself when dealing with God

– ' Yes, I think so ' – was God's firm and definitive answer

He let my soul to bounce back onto the table, somehow

rejuvenated

– ' I don't understand, what is it all about ? ' – I murmured

fearfully

afraid to be looking straight at God and His adversary

What was most surprising God Almighty just laughed

and all the stars on the Heavens' skies scintillated at the same

time

– ' It's nothing to do with you, Thaddeus, on my side. ' – God

said

– ' I just loved to be present in this scenery of the Carpathians

– ' Why then Satan's here, at this table ? ' – my soul asked

She did it courageously knowing God was her loving Father

– ' Yes, I know he had bad intentions. This is why he is here '

God answered my soul and then turned patiently to me

– ' You see, Thaddeus, you were looking for Dracula

at least you've been thinking of him. Satan's his best friend '

What could I answer about this revelation, so clear now to

me ?

– ' Thank you, God Almighty ' – I just said but felt relieved

God allowed me to smile to Him and even gifted me with His

smile

The next what I remembered were my candles snuffing out

one after another one while the stars were shimmering as

always

This time it was the symphony of the Phantom of the Night..

End Piece

About the Authors

Elluisa Conroy

My name is Elluisa Vargas and I was born and raised in Southern California. As a child I played the flute and was also a cheerleader. My English teacher from the 9th grade is who inspired me to write after reading a poem I had done in her class as a project. I have had a passion for writing since I was 15 years old.

Life inspires me to write. I helped put together The Poetry Alliance. I love and enjoy being part of The Poetry Alliance.

Thaddeus Hutyra

I was born in mountainous Rajcza, south Poland where I spent my childhood and teenager years, where I also studied and participated in the so called Solidarity movement against the communist regime.

I emigrated out of Poland just 8 days before the infamous martial law,   and became a citizen of New Zealand within five years. I lived in marvelous Wellington, the capital of NZ, called often ' Windy Wellington ', due to the very many winds blowing through the city both from the Pacific and nearby mountains. I lived there also in Auckland and Coromandel Peninsula for a while. Afterwards I traveled worldwide, been amongst others in China and finally settled down in Antwerp, Belgium.

I was already active on Facebook for some time, campaigning on human rights issues and dignity of individuals in various tyrannic dictatorships around the world when I got to know Ryan Christiano, a great writer, poet and human rights advocate.

It is he who persuaded me to join magnificent forum, The Poetry Alliance one and half a year ago, what resulted in writing by me one hundred poems during that time.

I wish to tribute Ryan Christiano for this and also all the great friends in this forum I am blessed to deal with.

Linde Griffis

Most of my childhood was spent moving around a lot with my dad's work. I claim to be a Cali girl as most of my childhood was spent there but I was born in Tulsa, Oklahoma. I spent 3 years in Germany in my early twenties while my first husband served in the Air Force. I am a mom of 4 and have been a nurse since 1997.

My passions today are natural healing, music, riding and being outdoors. I began writing in the midst of my last divorce. The poems came easy to me in such a time of questioning and moving forward from the loss. I have always desired to have my work published and am grateful for this amazing opportunity. My desire is that others may be able to heal as well by knowing that we are not alone in our travel through this life.

My involvement with The Poetry Alliance came about in a rather divine nature. I had gone to school with Ken but did not know him. Through Facebook I had found some old high school friends. I began searching groups on poetry. Since Ken was a founder of the poetry alliance and mutual friends, I was able to find the group of these fellow poets. The goal had always been to become published, which now we are seeing that come to pass. I am very thankful for the Poetry Alliance family.

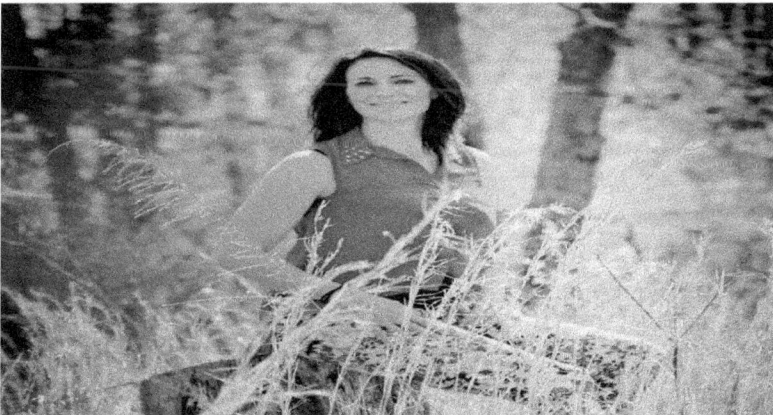

Alyson Rewick

Alyson was born and raised in New Jersey, and writing has always been one of her greatest passions. It allows her to have a voice, to interact with the world, and to leave her mark on history, small as it may be.

Rose Mary McKenzie

I'm from a Norther California town Ukiah,

a name give by the Pomo Indian nation.

As a teen I used to write poetry, but nothing serious.

I was blessed by Ken Blick inviting me to

join The Poetry Alliance after reading his poetry.

His encouragement started me on this beautiful road

of the written word, teaching me I could compose from

my heart and soul.

My inspirations comes from life lived, and love of my

eight grandchildren, friends and family, and God's nature.

It is an honor to be included with poets in The Poetry Alliance!

Ryan Christiano

Ana Vargas

Ana is a Mexican poetess residing in Vancouver, BC Canada. She began a spiritual awakening when her son was born.

The journey into her soul brought forth a spring of creativity reflected in her poems which speak to love, loss, suffering, survival, sacrifice and ultimately her path to God. Becoming accustomed with her voice, she joined the Poetry Alliance in order that it is heard by open souls.

Joy Blevins

I was born and raised in the Heartland of the US. I spread my wings to California as a young adult and found myself working with a contracting Company where we specialized in catering to the wealthy and famous.

I eventually moved back to the Heartland where I met the man of my dreams, married, raised our children and continue to live a peaceful, happy life. I began writing poetry in my early teens and continue to this day, drawing my inspiration from my family, friends and surroundings.

I joined The Poetry Alliance group a little over a year and a half ago I never imagined such a small group could welcome you with such big open arms. I am proud to call each and every one of them a dear friend. A very special thank you to Ken Blick, you saw my potential, brought me into this group and you continue to believe in me no matter what. I feel my life has been truly blessed in so many ways.

Joy

Ken Blick

I was raised in the small town of Mojave, California. I started writing poetry in high school as extra credit in English class. My teacher was impressed and said I should send them in for publication. I was more interested in traveling the world, so when I turned eighteen I joined the Army. I loved serving my country and seeing the world.

After eight years and thousands of miles later, I left the service and settled in Nebraska, the home of the good life. I never stopped writing poetry, I just never shared it with anyone.

When I joined Facebook, I shared a few poems and more and more people liked them, and I was again told I should have them published. Elluisa Granath–Vargas Conroy, through mutual friends, saw my poetry and we started talking. We hit it off and decide to create a group where we could share our works without being plagiarized. We shared a love of poetry and a desire to one day see our works in print.

During our collaboration, we found a few more people that shared our dream and together we truly became an alliance and a family. This book is more than a culmination of poetry, it's the answer to a journey that started for many of us, years and years ago.

It has been my great pleasure to have been involved in this endeavor and getting to know the wonderful poets that have made this book possible.

The Poetry Alliance

www.ingramcontent.com/pod-product-compliance
Lightning Source LLC
Chambersburg PA
CBHW051825040426
42447CB00006B/378